D1158966

UNASHAMED

Tim Fortner

First Printing: Unashamed
Author: Tim Fortner
© 2022
All rights reserved.

This book or parts thereof may not be reproduced in any form, stored in a retrieval system, or transmitted in any form by any means without prior written permission of the author, except as provided by United States of America copyright law.

Cover Art and Design: Eleos Press
www.eleospress.com

Interior Formatting: Eleos Press
www.eleospress.com

All Scripture, unless otherwise noted, comes from the New International Version, Zondervan, and King James Version of the Holy Bible.

ISBN-13: 9798409530563

PRINTED IN THE UNITED STATES OF AMERICA

FOREWORD

I first met Tim some twenty years ago and it is without reservation, I can say that Tim Fortner is a fully-devoted follower of Christ, a gifted Bible teacher, and communicator. He has faithfully served as an adult Bible study teacher at West Jackson Baptist Church for nearly twenty years until he recently relocated his family to Memphis, TN. His life and teaching give evidence that he is an approved worker who does not need to be ashamed, correctly teaching the word of truth. Over the years, Tim and I have had an ongoing conversation about how God is at work around us and how we can better respond to His invitation to join Him in His work.

This book may be just that invitation for you!

Did you know that *more* Americans are now over the age of 60 than under 18? This over age 60 demographic may include you, if not, indeed a person you know. The implication of this reality for Christians is that the number of aging followers of Christ has the unprecedented opportunity to give a vision of God to the generations following them. Expanding this vision is absolutely essential. Let's join together in capturing these decades for Christ before they slip from our grasp.

In these pages, Tim takes us to the precipice to look to the next horizon, to a place where we can glance back on history while at the same time gazing forward, anticipating life's trajectory as we move into the future. Tim uses American history as the context and His story as the foundation for the reader to view, evaluate, realign and record their own life stories. All for the ultimate purpose of providing an impact on their family - a life story, their legacy of the gospel. "This will be written for the generation to come, that a people not yet created may praise the Lord." Psalm 102:18

In these pages, you will find a resource to arm yourself and your family with courage and the truths revealed in the Scripture. You will also be presented with a practical tool to record the greatest gift you can leave your family – your testimony as to how you came

i

to know Christ as Savior and Lord. This tool will allow you to include stories from your life and the lessons you have learned, and the pivotal moments in your life where the Lord intervened and you learned an important truth. This is your opportunity to create a legacy, a tradition, and a family treasure. This is the legacy of His story we want to leave for the generations.

I wholeheartedly recommend this book and implore you to read and respond to His invitation to you to join the ranks of the **Unashamed**!

Lonnie L. Sanders,
Pastor of Mature Adult Discipleship and Church Assimilation
West Jackson Baptist Church, Jackson TN

TABLE OF CONTENTS

THE GREAT AWAKENING

America in 2021 is on the brink of losing sight of its Christian heritage upon which our country was founded. To understand the story of America and how it came to be, one must study the Great Awakening of the 1700's. The term "woke" has come to be associated with the BLM and Cultural Marxism movements. The word, woke, initially was the past tense of wake. Wake is defined as "to emerge from a state of sleep" (Webster's Dictionary). Today "woke" means to be well-informed and alert to racial or social injustice as defined by the current culture.

In Romans 13:11-14, Paul writes: "And to this, knowing the time, that now it is high time to awake out of sleep; for now, our salvation is nearer than the day we first believed. The night is far spent, and the day is at hand. Therefore, let us cast off the works of darkness, and let us put on the armor of light. Let us walk properly, as in the day, not in revelry and drunkenness, not in lewdness and lust, not in strife and envy. But put on the Lord Jesus Christ and make no provision for the flesh to fulfill its lust."

In 1739, the 13 British Colonies stretched from Maine to Georgia, more than 1400 miles (about half the width of the United States.) The 13 colonies had little to do with each other separated by distance, commerce, customs, religious differences, and interests. Each colony operated on its own, under the watchful eye of their British owners.

We were taught in school in my era the story of the Pilgrims and Puritans and the vital importance of their Christian faith. Their faith was the reason many had come to the new land to worship the God of the Bible in Spirit and Truth and freedom. But by the 1730's their religious zeal had diminished by the tremendous effort it took to sustain life and establish a civilization in this new country.

The Great Awakening was led by Reverend Jonathan Edwards, the best theologian among the group which included John and Charles Wesley who formed the Methodist denomination. But the "rock star" of the group was George Whitfield, the 24-year-old Church of England evangelist. He was the Billy Graham of his time.

When Whitfield first arrived in Philadelphia, his reputation had preceded him, helped in part by Benjamin Franklin's favorable articles of him in his Philadelphia Gazette. Franklin and Whitfield would become lifelong friends. Franklin promoted him in his paper and covered his revivals. Billy Graham had the support of William Randolph Hearst and his national papers when Graham's revival in Los Angeles in 1949 began to draw large crowds. An example of how the media can promote and spread good news, literally.

When George Whitfield arrived in Philadelphia in 1739, 4000 citizens showed up to get a glimpse of this renowned evangelist. To their surprise, young George Whitfield was of a slight build and cross-eyed. But God had gifted George Whitfield with a voice which could be clearly heard at great distances. It was rumored you could hear his voice at a mile's distance under the right circumstances. In 1739-1740, Whitfield would preach 350 times and travel 5,000 miles (about twice the width of the United States). His remarkable voice, his exciting, enthusiasm and gospel centered preaching drew tens of thousands of people to hear this phenomenal young man. He would come to America 13 times. In his life, Whitfield would preach more than 30,000 times. He died in 1770 at the age of 56. Whitfield had preached two hours the night he died with an attack of asthma.

By the time he died, George Whitfield was the most well-known individual in the 13 colonies. The four men, Jonathan Edwards, John & Charles Wesley, and George Whitfield, along with many unknown local pastors, had done what nothing else had been able to do—unite these 13 colonies. It is estimated 80% of the people were Christians and/or had a reverence for the Bible and God. They were united as "one body, one Spirit just as you were called to one hope and to one Lord, one faith, one baptism, one God and Father of all, who is over all and through all and in all" (Ephesians 4:4-6). Perhaps this explains the American Motto found on our money: e pluribus Unum—"out of many, one."

It was this mood and attitude which led to a revolution and a new country with a new form of self-rule government, the United States of America. Truth was defined by the Holy Bible, and was the recognized source of absolute truth which also determined our values.

Now you know the beginning of our story, let us explore what has happened since then with an eye on our past, present, and future.

OUR FORGOTTEN HISTORY

In the summer of 1787, in Philadelphia at Independence Hall, our founding fathers created the Constitution of a new country. The outcome of the work of these brilliant men was a new form of government of self-rule. It was a government by the people, for the people, and of the people. Sometimes we need to be reminded of what the hallmark of a republic form of government is—consent of the governed.

As they were leaving on the last day having finished the exhausting work of what turned out to be a miraculous 4200–word document, a question was asked of Benjamin Franklin. A lady asked the 81-year-old Franklin, "What have we got? A monarchy or a republic?" Franklin's reply was overheard by another delegate named, McHenry, who recorded Franklin's reply: "A republic, madam, if you can keep it?"

Eric Metaxas in his book, *If You Can Keep It*, writes: "Americans in the 21st century have a profound disconnect in our relationship to our country and its history." The movement to rewrite our history is not only alive and well it is flourishing in our schools across the country. We, as the elder generation, need to reconnect our children and grandchildren with the history of our country and its Christian Heritage.

Founding fathers and the heroes of the past are being vilified. Their monuments are being torn down, their names removed from schools, institutions, and buildings. There is a powerful cultural uprising which we have witnessed in the last two years, which coupled with the deadly COVID pandemic has brought rapid and unprecedented change. This new culture draws its ideology from Marxism. Spokespersons for this movement have stated their goal is to destroy this system of government and fundamentally change America.

I do not disagree there are problems in our society. I do disagree with the diagnosis and treatment. The source of social injustice, racism, sexual immorality, drugs, and crime are not caused by our system of government, they are caused by the human heart where evil and sin exist. The solution to our problems is Jesus Christ and His redeeming work. The answer is the Gospel, the Good News. Without God there is no reason to say "no" to anything. Without God, life makes no sense.

Tim Fortner

THIS IS OUR STORY

An inheritance is different from a legacy. An inheritance is something left FOR somebody, as defined by a legal will. It includes monies, property, heirlooms to be divided among the heirs. A legacy is something left IN somebody. A principle, truths, something you have taught and lived out before your family and those who know you. It is what your family would say, you were known to stand for and stand on.

The purposes of this book are to arm yourselves and your families with courage and truth as revealed in scriptures. We must remember, it was upon God's Word America was founded. These truths and principles are a precious part of our history and legacy. They are now under attack.

This book is also about your family history. There will be room in the back of this book for you to include your family's history. It will include stories from your life and the lessons you have learned. Pivotal moments when the Lord intervened, and you learned an important truth. We want to leave a legacy which says: "On Christ the Solid Rock I stand, all other ground is sinking sand." This will be a family legacy which one day your grandchildren will read and pass on to their grandchildren.

Most of us at our age, having lost our parents and grandparents wished we had asked them more questions about their lives than we did. Do not make this mistake. This is your opportunity to leave a legacy and create a tradition and a family treasure.

"This will be written for a generation to come, that a people not yet created may praise the Lord. "(Psalm 102:18)

Teach them this truth and unwavering source of guidance, the Word of God: "All scripture is given by inspiration of God and is profitable for doctrine, for reproof, for correction, for instruction in righteousness, that the man of God may be complete, thoroughly equipped for every good work" (2 Timothy 2:16, 17).

What America has lost can be found and restored by following the commands and principles found in God's Word. This is a spiritual battle which must be fought with spiritual weapons. Arm yourselves and your families with these spiritual weapons which are mighty and divine.

Onward Christian Soldiers!

Tim Fortner

THE CRISIS IN 1776

American officially declared war on Great Britain on July 4, 1776, with a document which we cherish, The Declaration of Independence. The declaration was greeted with cheers and celebrations, which soon turned to gunfire and death. Freedom comes at a price, and the young, ill-equipped country would soon find itself the underdog in a fight for its very existence.

Just weeks after declaring their independence, America suffered a humiliating defeat and lost New York City to the superior British army. By December, General Washington knew his army was in serious trouble. The winter weather was harsh; supplies were scant; their hopes diminishing. Volunteers were leaving in masses. Washington was left with an enlisted army whose enlistment ran out on January 1st—just a few short weeks ahead.

On December 19, 1776, a pamphlet appeared on the streets of Philadelphia, containing an essay authored by Thomas Paine. Paine had been with Washington and his forces and told Washington he would write something to help the troops' morale. The impact of the following short message was nothing short of a miracle.

"These are the times which try men's souls. The summer soldier and the sunshine patriot will, in this crisis shrink from the services of his country. But he that stands it now deserves the love and thanks of man and woman. Tyranny, like hell, is not easily conquered; yet we have this consolation with us, the harder the conflict, the more glorious the triumph. For what we obtain too cheaply, we esteem, too lightly; for it is dearness that gives everything its value. "

Washington had this message read to all his troops. Then on a bitter, cold Christmas Eve, 1776, Washington rallied his forces and crossed the icy Delaware River. On December 25, 1776, the ragtag American forces soundly defeated the Hessian Armies stationed there at Trenton, N.J. A week later, General Washington defeated General Cornwallis at Princeton and the war took a pivotal turn. Inspired by the words of Thomas Paine and the courage of their leader, General George Washington, this young country in-the-making had found its just cause.

THE CRISIS IN AMERICA IN 2020-21

In January of 2020, an invisible enemy entered silently across our borders. This enemy would later be identified as COVID-19, a deadly and contagious virus, which spread rapidly and created havoc around the world. At times it closed everything from businesses to churches. Armed with vaccines, masks, and social distancing, we are still fighting this virus after two years. In May of 2020 in Minnesota a man named, George Floyd, was brutally killed by the arresting officer. It was captured on numerous cell phones by bystanders and soon was being shown around the world. Soon the streets and cities in America were aflame with rioters protesting this horrendous event. Businesses were being burned and looted; whole sections of cities taken over and lives were being lost and turned upside down.

We are still at this point a nation of rage.

A review of the last 50 years will reveal how America and Americans have forgotten their history; how Christians have forgotten our leader, the Lord Jesus Christ, the Commander of the armies of heaven and His last command to us: "All authority has been given to me in heaven and earth. Go ye therefore and make disciples of all nations, baptizing them in the name of the Father, the Son, and the Holy Spirit, teaching them to observe all things I have commanded you. And lo, I am with you always until the end of the age" (Matthew 28:18-29).

Our enemy is the same one who entered the Garden of Eden and set about to destroy the family which God has created. Family was God's focus, His plan on how he would pass on truth, wisdom and understanding from one generation to the next. Parents and grandparents were to instruct their children in the ways of God to equip them for living a God-honoring life. Our generation is at the same place as the generation; Moses was preparing to enter the Promised Land in his farewell address recorded in the book of Deuteronomy.

Those of us who are of the Baby Boomer generation have become the elder generation. We are coming to the end of an era, and we cannot go where the next generation is going—into the future. But we can equip them with the truth and the spiritual weapons they will need in a culture which wants to erase our country's Christian Heritage and cancel their Christian faith and the nuclear family.

Here is where we are, as we read this ominous message following Joshua's death: "So the people served the Lord all the days of Joshua, and all the days of the elders who outlived Joshua, who had seen the great works of the Lord which He had done for Israel." Joshua died as age 110 and was buried and soon after that the generation of elders died out and we read in Judges 2: "There arose another generation after them who did not know the Lord nor the work which he had done for Israel." Everyone did what was right in their own eyes. We live in a country where everyone wants to do what is right in their own eyes. Rights without responsibilities.

In every generation there is a progression of the Gospel to the future which passes from the past through the present. Will the progression of the Gospel continue through history because of the role you are currently playing in your time slot? Or will the progression stop with you?

We are to be about our father's business. Jesus came to show us how this worked. This is your father's business which you and I are to be about. Jesus taught it, modeled it, and handed it over to 12 very ordinary men. It is described in the Gospels of Matthew, Mark, Luke, and John. We see the successful application of His teaching, which they duplicated in the book of Acts. The Great Commission is given to us by Jesus, along with His Power and His Presence in the Person of the Holy Spirit in Matthew 28:18-20. "All power has been given to Me in heaven and earth. Go ye therefore and make disciples in all nations, baptizing them in the name of the Father, the Son and the Holy Spirit, teaching them to observe all the things I have commanded you, and lo I am with you always until the end of the age."

Here is the question: Will courage skip a generation? God Forbid!

FOCUS ON THE FAMILY

James Dobson had it right: we must focus on our families, first. To fail to do so is to not arm them for the battles which lie ahead.

When Moses began to teach the next generation about to enter the Promised land, he began with the history of Israel and God's role in their country. He did not want them to forget their history and where they came from. I believe we must remember our history in America. But also, we must remember our origin, going all the way back to Genesis and Creation. One needs to know where they came from, why they are here, how to decide right from wrong, and what is our destination.

If one does not know where they came from, why they are on this journey, how to decide which way to go, or what their destination is; this is the very definition of being lost.

"Is life a tale told by an idiot, full of sound and fury, signifying nothing," as Hamlet opined? What a dark and depressing view of life. Longfellow wrote: "Tell me not in mournful numbers, life is but an empty dream, and the soul is dead that slumbers and things are not as they seem. Life is real, and life is earnest, and the grave is not the goal, dust thou art to dust returneth was not spoken of the soul."

Life is meaningless without God. Teach them they were created by God and for God. God has a plan for their lives. Once you know your purpose, the decision process is simplified: the action you are considering either aids you in achieving your purpose or not. Jesus said He came to testify to the truth. He said to those who believed, "If you abide in My Word, you are my disciple, indeed, and you shall know the Truth and the Truth shall set you free" (John 8:31, 32).

The enemy has been focused on the family since the Garden of Eden. His method has not changed. He lures with the following threesome: lust of the flesh, lust of the eyes, and pride of life. Marriage, as God defined, it is between a woman and a man, for life. Marriage as God intended it to be, creates family as God intended it to be. Family is the backbone of society. So goes the family, so goes the community and the nation.

Mankind was created in God's image and likeness. We were made and exist to rule and reign with God under His authority. We were to multiply and reproduce and fill the earth. But things are NOT AS GOD INTENDED THEM TO BE. A review of the last 50 years reveals an all–out attack on the family. In the last 50 years, divorce rates have doubled. This is true of professed Christians as well as non-believers. Watch the fallout from this destruction of family: teen suicides have tripled; violent crime has grown fourfold; causing prison population to increase fivefold; and out-of-wedlock births to increase six fold; and cohabitation without marriage has increased sevenfold.

In 1963, prayer was taken out of school. God was expelled. In 1973 the Supreme Court decreed and abortion was the right of every woman. Then it should come as no surprise, in 2015 the Supreme Court legalized same sex marriage.

This defiant act against God's plan and intentions for marriage, the foundation of family, was legalized in America. This law was celebrated across the nation including from the White House where the President ordered a rainbow of lights be shown upon the White House, thus using a covenant symbol given by God to celebrate the debauchery of mankind who want to do what is right in their own eyes.

"Cultural Marxism seeks to capture five cultural institutions in America which include: the social, political, educational, religious and, most importantly, the nuclear family" (We Will Not Be Silenced, Edwin Lutzer, Harvest House Publishers, page 22).

Family, which God created and ordained, is clearly the target of a relentless enemy.

HOW DID THIS HAPPEN IN AMERICA?

History reveals kingdoms and kings' rise and fall. As Christians we must remember we have dual citizenships. We are citizens of this country, the United States of America. We are also citizens of the Kingdom of God.

Here is what history reveals precedes the fall of nations: the more the government's role, the more the government's control. We have allowed the government to take control of certain areas we did not want to take on as our responsibility. Today we live in a culture hostile to Christianity and the Word of God. They have expelled God from the schoolroom, and banned Him from the workplace and the market. He is not welcome in the halls of Congress. As a result, we celebrate what we used to condemn, and condemn what we used to celebrate.

In the 1970's, Francis Schaeffer wrote, "One day we will wake up and realize the America we once knew was gone." Is that day here yet? Or do we have a chance to turn things around?

Our parents and grandparents, the Joshuas and Calebs of the 20th century have been called "the Greatest Generation of the 20th century." They endured two world wars, plus the Korean War and Vietnam. In between they had the Great Depression of the 1930's. Remember what we quoted earlier from Thomas Paine? "What we obtain too cheaply, we esteem too lightly. It is dearness that gives everything its value." They fought hard, worked hard and some gave their all for us to have what was handed to my generation on a silver platter.

We must be about our Father's business to prepare the next generations for what lies ahead for them.

Telling the American story is our responsibility. Fortunately, it is a short story, as far as histories of nations go. Less than 250 years old, we can get back to our birth as a nation quickly (My great grandfather's grandparents were born around the time our country was writing our constitution).

Tim Fortner

The debate about whether our country was founded on Biblical principles is easily refuted by the actual diaries and handwritten notes archived in our Library of Congress. Consider this fact: James Madison, the architect of the Constitution found the principles for our three separate branches of government in Isaiah 33:22: "For the Lord is our Judge, the Lord is our Lawgiver, the Lord is our King." They are: the judicial, legislative, and executive.

One of my favorite stories comes from a speech in July of 1787, which James Madison recorded for our knowledge. The constitutional convention was at a deadlock over congressional representation. Listen to these words of wisdom from Franklin and put to rest the untruth, this nation was not founded on Biblical principles and truths. Here are the words of Franklin: "In this assembly groping, as it were, in the dark to find a political truth, and scarce able to distinguish it when presented to us, how has it happened, that we have not once thought of humbly applying to the Father of Lights to illuminate our understanding? In the beginning of the war with Great Britain, when we were sensible of danger, we had daily prayer in this room for divine protection. Our prayers were heard, and they were graciously answered. All of us who were engaged in this struggle must have observed the frequent instances of superintending Providence in our favor."

To that kind of providence, we owe this happy opportunity of consulting in peace on the means of establishing our future felicity. And now have we forgotten our Powerful Friend? Or do we now imagine that we no longer need his assistance? I have lived a long time, and the longer I live, the more convincing proofs I see this truth: God governs in the affairs of men. And if a sparrow cannot fall to the ground without His notice, is it probable an empire cannot rise without His aid? We have been assured by the sacred writing, "unless the Lord builds a house, those who build it, labor in vain" (Psalm 127). I firmly believe without His concurring Aid, we shall succeed in this political building, no better than the builders of the Tower of Babel. We shall be divided by our little, partial, local interests; our projects confounded, and we ourselves will be a reproach and byword down to future ages. And what is worse, mankind may hereafter from this unfortunate instance despair of establishing governments by human wisdom and leave it to chance, war, and conquest. I therefore beg leave from these deliberations to move that henceforth prayers imploring the assistance of heaven and its blessings on our deliberations be held in this assembly every morning before we proceed with business by one or more of the clergies of this city" (The Debates in the Federal Conventions, Oxford Press, 1920).

I can hear the passion in Benjamin Franklin's voice 234 years later. These men understood the principle of leverage. They placed the lever of prayer on the fulcrum of the Word of God and reached all the way into heaven for the assistance of our High Priest, the Lord Jesus to intervene and created a new country. Prayer based on the Word of God gave these men the wisdom they asked for and enabled them to create a new form of government based on God's Word and Truth. One can also see a clear picture of our leadership today, which is described by Franklin as "groping in the dark to find a political truth, who imagine they do not need the assistance of God."

We drifted from these principles which were once so important that leaders of our country would stop to pray for guidance in important matters. The principle of drifting is we not only drift from something, but we also drift toward something. We have drifted away from what we were taught. As a result, we live in the midst of a corrupt and perverse society. Our parents and grandparents handed us a flaming torch of liberty.

The winds of indifference, apathy, neglect, and compromise have reduced it to a flickering candle. We are called to be salt and light. Light dispels darkness. Light is to be a beacon of hope in a world searching so hard for hope. We are called to be salt: salt hinders corruption, creates thirst, and adds flavor. We have forgotten our history, our heroes, and what made America great— their faith in God. We pledged allegiance to the flag of the United States and the Republic for which it stands, one nation under God, indivisible, with liberty and justice for all. We have let the enemy divide us. We have let the things of this world lure us away.

Tim Fortner

We must fight for something higher than ourselves, for not just what is ours, but for what should belong to everyone. To fight for what we know as Christians is right. Wake up, Christians, and strengthen what remains before it dies!"

LESSONS FROM MOSES: HOW TO EQUIP THE NEXT GENERATIONS FOR THE FUTURE

Moses is one of the best-known characters in the Bible. His story is so appropriate for us at this time in our lives. The book of Deuteronomy contains Moses' farewell address and teaching to the nation of Israel as they prepare to enter the Promised Land without Moses.

This series of sermons is his final instructions to this new generation which will enter the Promised Land after their wandering in the wilderness for 40 years, a generation. Moses was 120 years old. Moses spent his first forty years as a prince of Egypt. He learned the ways and wisdom of the Egyptian culture. Some believe he could have been the next Pharaoh. His first call was to be trained and equipped with knowledge he would later need to lead his people. His second calling came when Moses discovered his true heritage as an Israelite, and he wanted to help his people who were enslaved by the Egyptians. As a result, Moses intervened in the punishment of an Israelite slave and killed the Egyptian slave master.

This led to his leaving Egypt as a felon, wanted for murder and took him on the backside of nowhere in Midian, where Moses would spend the next 40 years as a shepherd working for his father-in-law. His third calling came when Moses was 80 years old. He turned aside to see a bush which was on fire, but not consumed. This led to his third calling which Moses was reluctant to answer, but he did, and the rest is history. What has God prepared you for in this time in your life? Are you asking Him?

To prepare this next generation for a future living among a radically different culture, Moses teaches them the history of the nation of Israel. He then teaches the 10 Commandments. One of the most important chapters in Deuteronomy is chapter 6 where Moses gives clear instructions to parents and grandparents. "Hear O Israel: The Lord our God is one! You shall love the Lord your God with all your heart, with all your soul, with all your strength. And these words, which I command you today shall be in your heart. You shall teach them diligently to your children and shall talk of them when you sit in your house, when you walk by the way, when you lie down, and when you rise up. You shall bind them as a sign on your hand, and they shall be as frontlets between your eyes. You shall write them on the door posts of your house and on your gates. "(Deut. 6:4-9)

Moses' goal was to teach and educate the people what they had to do to conquer the enemy, claim their promised inheritance, and live successfully in their new home to the glory of God. Consider the importance of the book of Deuteronomy: Jesus quoted from this book more than any other book in the Old Testament. Parents and grandparents, no long lectures, but short appropriate stories from your life, stories of how the Lord has intervened in your life and taught you lessons. Sprinkle Bible verses, like salt at the dinner table or at lunch with a grandchild.

RECONNECTING TO AMERICA'S HISTORY

Warren Wiersbe writes: "A grasp of history is important to every generation because it gives a sense of identification. If you know who you are and where you came from you will have an easier time discovering what you should be doing" (Be Equipped: Acquiring Tools for Spiritual Success, Victor Books, pages 15, 16).

If you want to know how far we have come in losing our identity, look at one of the most controversial topics in today's culture: gender identity. I am not going to meander off into a discussion of this, but just say what the Bible says: "So God created man in His own Image, in the image of God, He created him; male and female He created them" (Genesis 1:27).

When a nation loses its history, it loses its identity. Then it becomes what the people say it is. And as you can see, it becomes what the loudest, angriest voices say it is.

Has America as a country made mistakes? Yes, appalling ones—including slavery. But what those who are condemning us leave out is what we have done as Americans to correct what we have done wrong as best as we can. Pick any nation in the world and go back in their history and you will find behavior of which they are embarrassed, mortified sometimes the depths their nations have sunk at times, as in Germany in World War II.

To end slavery in the USA, we fought our most costly war in terms of loss of American lives. From 1861 to 1865, 620,000 Americans died in the war to end slavery. We lost more lives in this war, than in World War I, World War II, Korea, and Vietnam combined. The bloodiest battle ever fought was at Gettysburg, where 58,000 Americans died in three days. On July 3, 1863, President Abraham Lincoln delivered his famous Gettysburg Address: "Four Score and seven years ago, our fathers brought forth on this continent, a new nation, conceived in liberty, and dedicated to the proposition, that all men are created equal. Now we are engaged in a great civil war, testing whether that nation or any nation so conceived and dedicate can long endure." Is this not where we find ourselves in 2021? We as Christians can no longer be silent. When lies are told, when good is called evil, and evil good we must speak the truth in love.

COMPETING IDEOLOGIES

Victor Hugo, said, "There is one thing stronger than all the armies of the world, an idea whose time has come." Ideas have consequences.

Some will classify ideologies as political agendas. However, politics is a lagging indicator of where we are as a nation. This would explain why in the late 1990's under President Clinton and an equally divided congress of Democrats and Republicans passed the Defense of Marriage Act, which was to protect marriage as between a man and a woman. This was overturned 15 years later when same-sex marriage was legalized.

Other worldviews are described, as liberal, moderate, or conservative—each of which is continually being redefined. As a result, we have the pressure of political correctness, intolerance for viewpoints which differ and a state of continual chaos.

Karl Marx was trained as an economist, in the mid 1800's in liberal colleges in France. His ideology was based on defining the oppressors and the oppressed and dividing the populace into one of those two groups. Socialism always inevitably morphs into communism. He selected the impoverished as an oppressed group and capitalism as the problem. Socialism would solve the problems of racism, sexism, crime, and inequality. The government will own everything; no one could own private property. Everyone would share equally as determined by the government. When the government is looked to for all needs, it becomes the god. Government run schools, with their designed curriculum, are important parts of Marxism. This allows them to indoctrinate the children and teach them to believe what they teach.

Social media, propaganda, entertainment, Big Tech, are all tools used to change the future by rewriting our history.

Listen to Jesus' agenda which He presents at the beginning of His ministry at his hometown synagogue (recorded in Luke 4): "The Spirit of the Lord is upon Me, because He has anointed Me to preach the Gospel to the poor; He has sent me to heal the brokenhearted, to proclaim liberty to the captives, and recovery of sight to the blind, to set at liberty those who are oppressed; to proclaim the acceptable year of the Lord." He did not come to divide, but to unite. To not identify the oppressor and the oppressed, but set at liberty the oppressed.

Jesus sums up the difference between these two ideologies simply with this statement: "The thief comes to steal and kill and destroy, but I have come that you might have life and might have it more abundantly" (John 10:10).

"Of all the words of tongue or pen, the saddest of these—it might have been. "John Greenleaf Whittier.

The enemy is an identity thief. He wants to steal your identity as an image bearer of God. He wants to kill marriages. He wants to destroy the traditional family, which was God's means of passing knowledge of Him and the truth and how to live life as God intended it to be lived.

He wants to destroy the traditional family and do away with Christianity completely, shackling the Word and persecuting us who proclaim it. But remember this: in all of the history of the church, the church always grows during persecution.

Our forefathers wanted to make sure our freedom of religion was protected from a government who wanted to control everything.

The First Amendment of the Bill of Rights added in 1791 reads as following: "Congress shall make no law respecting an establishment of religion or the prohibiting the free exercise, thereof; or abridging free speech, or of the press; or of the right of the people to peaceably assemble, and to petition the government for redress."

Notice there is no phrase which says separation of church and state. In fact, it prohibits the state from forming a state religion. It is not about just the freedom to worship it is about the freedom to exercise your religion—pray in public, proclaim it in the marketplace, and live it out to its fullest.

This is the story of American History and how we came to be the greatest civilization in the world for the last 200 years.

THE FIVE SECRETS OF LIVING

The Westminster Catechism's most well-known statement is: "The chief end of man is to glorify God and enjoy Him forever." It would seem glorifying God is one of the most important things we can do and is a function for which we were created. Wouldn't you like to know the secret of glorifying God?

Let us ask Jesus how do we glorify God? "By this is My Father glorified that you bear much fruit." (John 15:8)

Secret one. We glorify God by bearing fruit. This leads us to the question: how do we bear fruit?

Secret two. The secret to bearing fruit is abiding. "Abide in Me and I in you, as the branch cannot bear fruit of itself, unless it abides in Me (John 15:4). This makes perfect agricultural sense, apart from the vine, the branch cannot bear fruit.

Secret three. How do we abide is the question before us? The secret to abiding is obedience.

Secret four. What is our motivation for obedience? Jesus tells us: "If you love me, you will keep my commandments" (John 14:15).

Secret five. What is the secret to loving? Knowing. In John 17, Jesus says, "This is eternal life to know the true and living God and Jesus Christ whom You have sent."

There it is: the secret of living is fruit bearing; the key to fruit bearing is abiding; the secret to abiding is obedience. Obedience grows out of loving and loving comes from knowing. The more you know Him, the more you will love Him. And the more you love Him, the more you will obey Him. And the more you and I obey Him, the more we will abide in Him and bear more fruit. The secret of living and of experiencing the joy we were intended to enjoy.

("FIVE SECRETS OF LIVING," Warren Wiersbe, Tyndale Publishing) I strongly suggest you make this small book (88 pages) part of your library.

The reason God saved you is that you might bear fruit in this world. You and I are living in a hungry world, starving for the Truth, being fed lies.

THE PRINCIPLE OF SOWING AND REAPING

From the first chapter of Genesis, we see the agricultural principle of sowing and reaping. God created all things to reproduce after their own kind. The seed is an essential element and given special meaning in Genesis 3. God made a way for plants, birds, fish, creatures, and man to reproduce after their own kind.

"Be not deceived. God is not mocked; for whatever a man sows, that he will also reap. For he who sows to the flesh will, of the flesh, reap corruption, but he who sows to the Spirit will, of the Spirit, reap everlasting life. And let us not grow weary while doing good for in due season we shall reap if we do not lose heart. Therefore, as we have opportunity, let us do good to all, especially to those who are of the household of faith" (Galatians 6:7-10).

- The principles of sowing and reaping are clear.
- Principle of investment: you cannot reap if you do not sow.
- Principle of identification: you reap what you sow.
- Principle of increase: you reap more than you sow.
- Principle of interval: you reap later than you sow.
- Location: where we sow makes a difference. Sow to the flesh, the Spirit, or the wind.

How we sow impacts outcome: sow sparingly, reap sparingly; sow plentifully, reap plentifully.

THE ROLE OF THE DISCIPLE

One of the defining characteristics of a disciple as defined by Jesus is: "Then Jesus said to those disciples who believed in Him, 'If you abide in My word, you are my disciples indeed, and you shall know the truth and the truth shall set you free'" (John 8:31, 32). Teach this truth to your children and grandchildren.

A mental filter reinforced with Biblical truth is essential for Christians because it identifies things which align with the Word of God and rejects whatever is sinful, deceptive, and unwise or otherwise harmful to us.

A disciple is a follower of Jesus. Jesus' first invitation to a group of professional fishermen was, "Follow Me and I will make you fishers of men." Disciples are made. "Disciple" is not a label; it is a lifestyle. The goal of Jesus was to produce disciples who could make disciples. This meant they must become learners and teachers, continuous learning. Jesus modeled this strategy and curriculum to be used. It was a pattern of sound words they were to copy.

Jesus then sent His disciples out on missions so they could put into practice what they had been taught and observed Jesus doing. Teaching + training is critical for equipping one for the work of discipling.

Discipling is done by individuals not institutions. This is our responsibility, our job as members of the family of God. We must be about our Father's business. As a Christian who wants to imitate Christ, we are never more like Him, than when we are carrying out the Great Commission. Paul writes to Timothy and instructs him and us to do the following: "Hold fast to the pattern of sound words you have heard from me, in faith and love which are in Christ Jesus" (2 Timothy 1:13). Paul is referring to the Gospel. Paul gives us the four parts of the Gospel we must always hold fast to and not leave out any one of the parts. Christ died for our sins, according to the Scriptures, He was buried, and He rose again on the third day according to the Scriptures, and He was seen by more than 500 witnesses (I Corinthians 15:5).

Paul also wrote in his last letter to Timothy: "And the things that you have heard from me among many witnesses, commit these to faithful men who will be able to teach others" (2 Timothy 2:2).

This is the pattern of disciple making. The new believer must be taught the Word of God. He must be led by example. The new disciple must be trained to transfer the faith to others. In this way the Gospel has moved from the past to the present using this method which Jesus taught, from the past through the present to the future for more than 2,000 years to millions and millions of people in the world.

Paul compares us to soldiers who endure hardship and let nothing entangle us to keep us from the battle. He likens us to farmers who sow the seed and cultivate it, athletes who train to compete, vessels to be emptied of self to be filled with Him. And servants whose aim in life is to do the will of their master.

Tim Fortner

THE INCORRUPTIBLE SEED

The Seed has life in it. Peter says, "Having been born again, not of corruptible seed, but incorruptible seed through the Word of God which abides forever." (I Peter 1:23) James tells us we are saved by the implanted (engrafted) Word, which can save our souls. But James warns us: "For if anyone is a hearer of the Word and not a doer, he is like the man who looks in the mirror at his face, then goes away and forgets what kind of man he is. But he who looks in the perfect law of liberty and continues in it and is not a forgetful hearer, but a doer, this one will be blessed in what he does."

The Word of God is alive and powerful, sharper than a two-edged sword. It is life giving, life transforming and life sustaining. Read it to be wise, believe it to be saved. The Spirit of God uses the Word of God to make us like the Son of God. "All scripture is inspired by God and profitable for doctrine, reproof, correction instruction, so that the man of God may be perfect and thoroughly equipped for every good work" (2 Timothy 3:16, 17).

The Word of God is a light upon our path and a lamp unto our feet.

THE KEY TO SUCCESSFUL SOWING OF THE SEED

Everything takes time and effort. Remember there are no shortcuts to any place worth going. Here are five simple steps to engrafting the Word of God, using the "Word Hand" from Navigators.

- Hear the Word of God. Use your little finger, for we only retain 5% of what we hear. Yet faith comes by hearing and hearing by the Word of God (Romans 10).
- Read the Word of God. Use your ring finger for reading, which we usually retain 15% of what we read. Reading provided breadth and we read devotionally each morning.
- Study the Word of God. Use your middle finger for this requires more time and effort, but study results in up to 35% retention. 'Study to show yourself approved unto God, a workman who needs not to be ashamed, rightly dividing the Word of Truth (2Timothy 2:15). Study of the Word increases knowledge and deepens convictions.
- Memorize the Word of God. We use the index finger for it is the strongest. This is one of the most crucial elements of Bible intake. We use the Word of God to overcome temptations, and to counsel others.
- Meditation. We use the thumb to illustrate this process, for the thumb is the only digit which can touch and bring together the other fingers. By meditating on what we hear, read, study, and memorize, our minds are transformed. Meditation is also the connection between Bible intake and prayer.

FIVE MUST –BELIEVES.

- You must believe God is who He says He is.
- You must believe God can do what He says He can do.
- You must believe you are whom God says you are.
- You must believe you can do what God says you can do.
- The Word of God must be an integral part of your everyday life.

Are you familiar with the story of the man who had a son who had a mute spirit and suffered seizures which threw him to the ground, caused him to foam at the mouth and gnash his teeth? The disciples had been unable to do anything, so the man brings him to Jesus with this simple, earnest request: request: "If you can do anything, have compassion on us." To which Jesus replied, "If you can believe, all things are possible to him who believes." Immediately the father of the child cried out, "Lord, I believe; help my unbelief!" Jesus healed the boy immediately (Mark 9).

I love this story, so remember this prayer when your faith wavers, but you know Jesus wants to have compassion on you, ask Him to help your unbelief.

THE PURPOSE DRIVEN LIFE

"The Purpose Driven Life: What on Earth Am I Here For?" by Rick Warren, was first published in 2002. Its impact was almost immediate, and the fact it would go on to sell 34 million copies worldwide tells us it struck a nerve with the question in the subtitle: "What On Earth Am I Here For?"

Watching our children and grandchildren grow up, parents and grandparents look for natural talents and abilities and what interests their offspring, as to help direct them in finding what they want to do with their life. The Bible tells we were created by Him and for Him. This is where we will find our purpose. God is not just the starting point of your life; He is the source of life. You will discover your identity and purpose through a personal and intimate relationship with Jesus Christ. God chose the time and place you would be born. He chose your parents. "You are who you are for a reason. You're part of an intricate plan. You're a precious and perfect unique design, Called God's special woman or man" (Russell Kelfer).

God's Purpose for You

- You were planned for God's pleasure.
- You were formed for God's family.
- You were created to be like Christ.
- You were shaped for serving God.
- You were made for a mission

This book, "The Purpose Driven Life," by Rick Warren, Zondervan Publishing, should be in your library. It is a rich source of scripture and each of these five purposes are explained in detail.

It can be an excellent source for parents and grandparents alike to help their children and grandchildren find their way

THE HUMAN RACE

The human race is a relay race. If you are not familiar with track and field events, the relay race is a team sport. Four runners each run equal legs of the race. The sprints are the most common. For example, the 400-meter relay consists of four runners each running 100 meters. There are the starter, the 2nd man, the third and the anchor man. The first three runners are responsible for passing off to the next runner; the anchor man is the final runner who will cross the finish line.

The passing of the baton to the next runner on the team is a critical juncture in the relay race. The pass-off zone is a set distance of 21 meters. If you exceed the pass-off zone and pass it off outside of the zone, your team is automatically disqualified. If you drop the baton, the loss of time in the sprints usually means you will lose. Practice and training are necessary.

The 21 meters sound like ample space in which to make the exchange, but these are sprinters who can cover this distance in 2-3 seconds. In addition, the runner receiving the baton takes off before the runner enters the zone and the pass is a "blind pass," in that the one receiving the baton holds his hand behind him while looking and running forward.

This is a picture of the fast-paced life we live in the 21st century. We have a brief time with our children and grandchildren where we are the most important people in their lives. Remember when you were small? You thought your parents could solve any problem which came up in your life. They seemed to know the answer to everything and could take care of any problem you had. Those days my boys waited for me to come home from work so we could play football or basketball did not last long. Before long they were off to school, making friends and learning new things at school. Be sure to make the most of those days and times wisely, for they are fleeting and the days of evil are coming. Have family meals, no television or cell phones at the table.

Ask about their days, sprinkle some salt, and shed some light. A verse here and there, an interesting factoid, planting and cultivating and making sure of what they are learning and hearing from their instructors. Precept upon precept. An interesting story here and there.

Just like the runners, you must practice until it becomes second nature to introduce spiritual truths. Practice doesn't make perfect; it makes permanent.

This is legacy passing 101.

Tim Fortner

FOLLOW THE SCIENCE: THE TRUE SCIENCE OF GOD

In the last two years of the pandemic, we have heard this phrase time and time again: "Follow the science."

Science often scoffs at Christians who believe the Creation Account as recorded in Genesis. Know this: the generations to come will face ridicule from those who believe the Creation Account in Scriptures is a myth. Furthermore, they believe those who believe it are foolish and ignorant. This is happening now at our local public schools. Indoctrination into their philosophy which sometimes disguises itself as science is at work even in the elementary grades. Certainly, it will be faced on the college campuses as espoused as truth by the liberal professors.

I have discovered as a speaker, teacher, and writer, as well as a parent and grandparent, children and adults alike love stories and amazing facts. God invented science. His Science is true, and it is amazing. Let us explore how to use this true science to capture the attention of children, teenagers, and adults. Be creative, and also age- and gender-conscious.

God has given us evidence of His existence to every person on earth: "For since the creation of the world His invisible attributes are clearly seen and understood by the things that are made, even His eternal power and Godhead, so they are without excuse" (Romans 1).

Here are some amazing facts about creation, which never fail to grab one's attention. Believing the creation account is particularly important, for it is the foundation upon which Scripture rests. Science and its discoveries have done nothing to weaken the story; in fact, conversely, discoveries made as recently as the 20th and 21st century support the reality of a Creator of great intelligence and imagination. Everything we need for life and godliness was created in those first six days of creation. Mankind has taken thousands of years to discover what God knew we would need.

Green plants take in sunlight from the sun and turn water and carbon dioxide into oxygen which we breathe and is necessary for life and, as a byproduct, produces sugar which sweetens our lives and attracts bees, which cross-pollinate. So take a deep breath and thank a plant which was created by God and enables Him to provide us with the very air that we breathe. For it is God who is the God of photosynthesis.

Evaporation is a process which takes place continuously, which we seldom or rarely think about. Remember 3/4ths of the earth's surface is covered with water. Sunlight warms the surface of the water causing the molecules of H2O to move faster and turn into vapor which is drawn up into the air where it is stored in clouds. As the air cools, condensation takes place and comes back to earth in rain, which waters the plants, crops, and flowers.

Thank your Heavenly Father for evaporation, for without it we would be underwater.

Space and the endless heavens have been of interest to man from the beginning. We have seen the role sunlight play in life on earth. Light travels at 186,240 miles per second. How fast is that? Snap your fingers—light just went around the earth 7.5 times!

Our day star, the sun, is 93 million miles away. Our earth revolves around the sun. Our yearly orbit takes us 365.25 days, giving us our calendar year and our four seasons. Our annual journey covers 554 million miles. We rotate on our axis at 1,000 m.p.h., giving us our 24-hour day divided into daytime and nighttime. In our revolution around the sun, we average 67,000 m.p.h.

Stars in the infinite skies are so far away that their distance is measured in light years. A light year is how far light travels in a year at the speed of 186,240, miles per second. Don't reach for your calculator; it cannot compute this distance. A light year is 5.88 trillion miles. How much is a trillion? Let me give you a comparison based on time: a million seconds ago was 12 days ago; a billion seconds was 31 years ago; a trillion seconds was 31,288 years ago! FYI—the Milky Way is 100,000 light years from one side to the other!

The Bible tells us we are "fearfully and wonderfully made" (Psalm 139:14). The Psalmist continues with this: "Your eyes saw my substance, being yet unformed. And in Your book, they all were written, the days fashioned for me, when as yet there are none of them." In June of the year 2000, six months into the 21st century, the Human Genome team headed by Dr. Francis Collins, a Christian, broke the human genome code. The code contains the instructions for building a human life. It was an instruction book written in the cryptic code of DNA in an alphabet, which we call, A, C, G, and T. These letters are abbreviations for their chemical bases. In one cell this 4-letter code is arranged in a three billion letter sequence. It is a bounded set of instruction for building a human life in the womb from conception to birth, in an orderly time and fashion. The DNA sequences contain the instructions needed for the organism to develop. The DNA is converted into messages that can be used to produce proteins which are complex molecules used to do most of the work.

This book of instructions on how to build a human life is in each cell of the body in the form of a double helix of DNA. If this compact spiral were unwound, it would be approximately six feet in length. The exact number of cells in the human body is unknown. Estimates are from a low of 10 trillion up to 50 trillion. If we use the lowest estimate of cells at 10 trillion, if we took the DNA from each cell from your body it would reach from earth to the sun, (a distance of 93 million miles) back and forth multiple times!!

God then wrote another instruction book in our language called the Bible with instructions how to live the life He built!

We do not want to miss the miraculous life-giving source and importance of blood. Life is in the blood. Your heart beats on an average of 100, 000 times per day to keep 8 pints of blood flowing through the 60,000 miles (which would reach around the earth 2.5 times) of blood vessels, arteries, veins, and capillaries of the human body. Blood brings life to every cell in the human body, and at the same time cleanses by washing away dead cells and waste. Remember without the shedding of blood there is no remission of sins. As the old hymn says, "What can wash away my sins, nothing but the blood of Jesus."

Follow the God of Science, the Creator of all things. These fascinating facts always bring me to the point of worship of Almighty God the One and Only Creator, of whom "the heavens declare His glory. And the firmament shows His handiwork. Day unto day utters speech and, night unto night, reveal knowledge. There is no speech or language where their voices are not heard" (Psalm 19).

Now let me remind you and your family, your children, and grandchildren of this amazing promise. God the Father, Creator of heaven and earth and everything in it and on it, is speaking to you through all of this and here is the message He has left on your prayer voice mail:

"Call on Me, and I will answer you, and show you great and mighty things you do not know" (Jeremiah 33:3). Won't you call on Him today? Who would not like to have a personal, intimate relationship with the One who created you, loves you and gave His only Son for you?

EPILOGUE OF THE UNASHAMED

The following comes from the writings left behind of a young African martyr. It is a call to all of us to join the unashamed of all ages, as Apostle Paul, who wrote: "I am not ashamed of the Gospel of Christ, for it is the power of God unto salvation of all who believe, for the Jew first and also the Greek" (Romans 1:16). Paul was not ashamed of the Gospel socially, intellectually, or morally, and neither should we be. My prayer, as you read these words, is that you will be challenged to join the fellowship of the unashamed. Listen to these stirring words:

"I'm part of the fellowship of the unashamed, the die has been cast, I have stepped over the line, the decision has been made—I'm a disciple of Jesus Christ, I won't look back, let up, slow down, back away or be still!"

My past is redeemed, my present makes sense, and my future is secure. I am finished and done with low living, sight walking, smooth knees, colorless dreams, tamed visions, worldly talking, cheap giving and dwarfed goals."

My pace is set, my gait is fast, my goal is heaven, my road is narrow, my way is rough, my companions are few, my guide is reliable, my mission is clear. I won't give up, shut up, or let up, until I have stayed up, stored up and prayed up for the cause of Jesus Christ. I must go until He comes and when He comes for His own. He will have no trouble recognizing me because my banner will have been clear." ANONYMOUS AND UNASHAMED.

THE DAY MY STORY MET GOD'S STORY

The day I lost all hope of every being sober came on September 16, 1977. Hopelessness is a dark and desperate place. My life had not turned out as I intended. A 31-year-old alcoholic, straddling the rail on the balcony of my 10th floor hotel room, I intended to jump from there. But at the last moment I fell back into the room and cried out to the Lord Jesus this unforgettable prayer. "Lord Jesus, if you are real, come into the room and into my life and save me, or else I am going to die." The prayer of an honest doubter who wanted to know the truth. And the One who is called, the Way, the Truth, and the Life, saved me and became my life.

I like to picture this scene in my mind. Jesus presenting me to His Father, with His strong arm wrapped around my shoulder. The smile of joy on His face widens as He says one word: MINE! And ever since that day I have looked to the Lord Jesus to remind me of that day with one word—His!

Thus began the glorious journey 44 years ago.

Tim Fortner
LIVING THE UNASHAMED LIFE

Jesus gives clear instructions to us believers in the 21st century. Here are His words to us from Revelation 3: "And to the angel of the church in Sardis write: 'These things say He who has the seven spirits of God and the seven stars: I know your works that you have a name that you are alive, but you are dead. Wake up and strengthen the things which remain, that are ready to die, for I have not found your works perfect before God. Remember therefore how you have received and heard and hold fast and repent. Therefore, if you do not watch, I will come upon you as a thief, and you will not know what hour I come upon you.'"

Repeatedly in the Scripture we are told to be alert, diligent, and watchful. We are told to repent. To wake up. To hold fast to the pattern of sound words which we have heard, read, and been taught. We are to study the Word of God to show yourself approved. Focus on your family, your friends, your neighbors, and community.

America's lost Christian heritage will not be reclaimed through the political process, politicians, and the government. Chuck Colson said if you live by the political sword, you will die by the political sword (This does not mean to not be involved in the politics and the government, especially at the local level.). Realize God has left us here to be agents of change. We are ministers of reconciliation. We are ambassadors of God's Kingdom. We are a chosen people, a royal priesthood, a holy nation.

The Gospel, of which we are unashamed, is to be shared with those that God brings in our lives: family, friends, neighbors, and the many people we cross paths with each day. The Gospel must come from our lives and lips. Our task is simple to witness to the truth of the Gospel in *a nation under judgement.*

For such at times as this we came into the kingdom of God. We are to build our lives on the Rock and not act like we are hanging by a thread. Jesus said to those who hear these sayings of mine and do them, "I will liken them to the wise man who built his house on the rock. The storms, rains, floods, and winds blew, but the house stood. But everyone who hears these sayings of mine and does not do them will be like the foolish man who built his house on the sand: and the rain descended, and the floods came, and the winds blew and beat on that house; and it fell with a great fall" (Matthew 7:24-27).

"Unless the Lord builds the house, those who build it labor in vain" (Psalm 27). House refers to family, to life and what one builds their life on and around.

There is an urgency which the Lord Jesus is telling us to wake up and strengthen what remains. Prepare them for the future to live in a radically different culture which opposes the Word of God. We are called to be salt—that which hinders corruption, creates thirst, and adds flavor. We are called to be light in what is becoming a dark place spiritually.

Saul of Tarsus was a man driven by his obsession to stamp out Christianity. His direction in life changed with an encounter with the Lord Jesus Christ on the road to Damascus. Blinded by the light, Saul asked two especially important, life-changing questions of the Lord: "Who are you? What do you want me to do?" Saul of Tarsus became a new creation. He changed his name to Paul and became the apostle to the Gentiles and wrote half of the New Testament.

Paul's obsession was to know the Lord Jesus and make Him known. All his previous accomplishments and works, he now considered rubbish. Paul had a calling which redirected his life, his purpose, and his obsession. He was a man not given to half-hearted efforts. Whatever Paul did, he did with all his heart. By now, dear reader, you should have learned there are no shortcuts to any place worth going. Show me a successful person, and I will show you someone who understands the need of wholehearted efforts.

I had a friend whose life reminded me of this man, Saul of Tarsus, a.k.a., Paul the Apostle. John Hillis was a retailer extraordinaire. John was one of Sam Walton's superstore managers. Sam Walton recognized John's talents and expertise and valued his opinion. John told me 60-70 hours were not an unusual work week for him. He loved his work and like Paul, he only knew one way to do things, with wholehearted efforts. But health issues changed his directions. John Hillis became a Christian in his 50s. He had a new boss, and a new career. John went at it with the same intensity he ran a huge retail store. He had to now be about his Father's business and John even in poor health, found ways to share the Gospel every day, to encourage others, reach out to the homeless and encourage and feed them spiritually and physically. He reached out in many innovative ways. He had an obsession, a magnificent obsession.

John Hillis lived his life to his very last day, unashamed of the Gospel, for it is the power of God unto salvation to all who believe.

THE COLSON INSTITUTE

I am finishing my 10-month online course from the Colson Institute designed by the late Chuck Colson. It has been an intense study and it has led me to write this study and start this mission. My mission is targeted toward two specific groups: 14-18 –year-olds. I have a presentation for them entitled: Preparing for the 10 most important years in your life. I share my testimony and lead them down the Roman Road and the sinner's prayer. My other target is my generation, the Baby Boomer and leaving a legacy. Telling your own story, aided by this unique book: UNASHAMED.

The mission statement of the Colson Institute has become my mission also.

- Protect what is good.
- Oppose what is harmful.
- Supply what is missing.
- Restore what is broken.

I want to run the race set before me with endurance, looking unto Jesus, the author and finisher of my faith. Who for the joy set before Him, endured the cross, despising the shame and has set down at the right hand of God.

I would like to invite you to join me and Gina in the fellowship of the unashamed. I covet your prayers and involvement. We would love to hear from you.

Tim &Gina Fortner

Johntfortner@gmail.com

www.timfortner.com (Contains some of our Bible studies, plus access to YouTube presentations.

There are so many teachers, preachers and authors who have blessed me and continue to teach me. Nothing is a substitute for the Bible, but there are many books which have taught me and helped me in my journey (see the list below).

RESOURCES

HOW NOW SHALL WE LIVE?   Charles Colson & Nancy Pearcey, Tyndale House Publishing, 1999.

AMERICA'S GODLY HERITAGE. David Barton, Wall Builder Press, 1993.

BE EQUIPPED: ACQUIRING TOOLS FOR SPIRITUAL SUCCESS. Warren Wiersbe, Victor Books. 1999.

THE MASTER PLAN OF DISCIPLESHIP, Robert E. Coleman, Revell Publishing, 1987.

KNOWING GOD. J.I. Packer. IVP Books, 1993.

TALLY HO, THE FOX! Herb Hodges, Spiritual Life Ministries, 2001.

GOD AS HE LONGS FOR ME TO SEE HIM. Chip Ingram, Baker Books, 2006.
5 SECRETS OF LIVING, Warren Wiersbe, Living Books, Tyndale House, 1977.

THE PURPOSE DRIVEN LIFE. Rick Warren, Zondervan, 2002.

THE DIVINE CONSPIRACY. Dallas Willard, Harper Collins, 1998.

SAVING TRUTH. Abdu Murray, Zondervan, 2018.

WE WILL NOT BE SILENCED. Erwin Lutzer, Harvest House, 2020.

YOUR FAMILY TREE

As Christians, you have two family trees—for we are a peculiar people who are twice-born. Both our physical and spiritual genealogies are passed from one generation to the next. The following segment, dear reader, is where you are asked to fill in the blanks for your children, grandchildren, great-grandchildren and beyond regarding your family tree and its branches.

As Christians, our spiritual family tree is linked to the Day of Pentecost, 2000 years ago. Every Christian alive today is linked via a complex chain of historical events with all their twists and turns. It was upon this day, the Holy Spirit came to enter the lives of believers and create a new race of people. We are described as, "born again."

This description is not one given to us by evangelists, but by the Lord Jesus Christ. Jesus said to Nicodemus in one of the most important conversations ever recorded: "Most assuredly, I say to you, unless one is born again, he cannot see the kingdom of God." (We often use the word "see" to convey the idea of understanding). Jesus continues, "Most assuredly, I say to you, unless one is born again of water and the Spirit, he cannot enter the kingdom of God. That which is born of the flesh is flesh, and that which is born of the Spirit is spirit. Do not marvel that I said unto you, 'You must be born again.'" (John 3:3, 5-7)

Now it is your turn in the following pages to write your story: "This will be written for the generation to come, that a people yet to be created may praise the Lord" (Psalm 102:18).

MY MOTHER

My Mother's
Great-Grandmother

My Mother's
Great-Grandfather

_____

_____

My Mother's
Grandmother

My Mother's
Grandfather

_____

_____

My Mother's
Mother

My Mother's
Father

_____

_____

My Mother

_____

MY FATHER

My Father's
Great-Grandfather

My Father's
Great-Grandfather

_____

_____

My Father's
Grandfather

My Father's
Grandfather

_____

_____

My Father's
Mother

My Father's
Father

_____

_____

My Father

_____

MY MOTHER (an interview)

GROWING UP

Elementary school: _____

Friends: _____

_____

_____

Teachers: _____

_____

_____

Games you played: _____

_____

_____

Special memories: _____

_____

_____

_____

_____

TEENAGE YEARS

Junior High school: _____

High school: _____

High school friends: _____

_____

_____

High school sports: _____

_____

_____

High school activities: _____

_____

_____

_____

High school special memories: _____

_____

_____

_____

_____

STORIES ABOUT YOUR GRANDPARENTS

Time spent with them: _____

_____

_____

_____

Where did they live? _____

_____

_____

Special times with them: _____

_____

_____

_____

What you remember most about your favorite grandparents:

_____

_____

_____

_____

SPIRITUALITY, RELIGION AND FAITH—
tell me about your:

Faith: _____

_____

_____

Church: _____

_____

_____

_____

A special time in your life where the Lord intervened: _____

_____

_____

_____

_____

_____

Favorite Bible Verse(s): _____

_____

_____

WORK, CAREER AND EDUCATION

What jobs have you had? _____

_____

_____

_____

_____

_____

Were you in the military? _____

_____

_____

_____

College? _____

_____

_____

_____

_____

HOW YOU MET EACH OTHER AND YOUR WEDDING

Special times in your life: _____

_____

_____

_____

_____

Starting a family: _____

_____

_____

_____

_____

YOUR ADVICE TO US

What is the one thing you would want us to know and do? _____

_____

_____

_____

_____

_____

HOW WOULD YOU LIKE TO BE REMEMBERED?

What is the main thing which you want to be known for? _____

_____

_____

_____

_____

_____

_____

_____

_____

_____

_____

_____

_____

_____

_____

_____

_____

MY FATHER (an interview)

GROWING UP

Elementary school: _____

Friends: _____

_____

_____

Teachers: _____

_____

_____

Games you played: _____

_____

_____

Special memories: _____

_____

_____

_____

_____

TEENAGE YEARS

Junior High school: _____

High school: _____

High school friends: _____

_____

_____

High school sports: _____

_____

_____

High school activities: _____

_____

_____

_____

High school special memories: _____

_____

_____

_____

_____

_____

MY MOTHER (an interview)

GROWING UP

Elementary school: _____

Friends: _____

_____

_____

Teachers: _____

_____

_____

Games you played: _____

_____

_____

Special memories: _____

_____

_____

_____

_____

TEENAGE YEARS

Junior High school: _____

High school: _____

High school friends: _____

_____

_____

High school sports: _____

_____

_____

High school activities: _____

_____

_____

_____

High school special memories: _____

_____

_____

_____

_____

STORIES ABOUT YOUR GRANDPARENTS

Time spent with them: _____

_____

_____

_____

Where did they live? _____

_____

_____

Special times with them: _____

_____

_____

_____

What you remember most about your favorite grandparents:

_____

_____

_____

_____

SPIRITUALITY, RELIGION AND FAITH—
tell me about your:

Faith: _____

_____

_____

Church: _____

_____

_____

_____

A special time in your life where the Lord intervened: _____

_____

_____

_____

_____

_____

Favorite Bible Verse(s): _____

_____

_____

WORK, CAREER AND EDUCATION

What jobs have you had? _____

_____

_____

_____

_____

_____

_____

Were you in the military? _____

_____

_____

_____

_____

College? _____

_____

_____

_____

_____

HOW YOU MET EACH OTHER AND YOUR WEDDING

Special times in your life: _____

_____

_____

_____

_____

Starting a family: _____

_____

_____

_____

_____

YOUR ADVICE TO US

What is the one thing you would want us to know and do? _____

_____

_____

_____

_____

_____

HOW WOULD YOU LIKE TO BE REMEMBERED?

What is the main thing which you want to be known for? _____

_____

_____

_____

_____

_____

_____

_____

_____

_____

_____

_____

_____

_____

_____

STORIES ABOUT YOUR GRANDPARENTS

Time spent with them: _____

_____

_____

_____

Where did they live? _____

_____

_____

Special times with them: _____

_____

_____

_____

What do you remember most about your favorite grandparents:

_____

_____

_____

_____

SPIRITUALITY, RELIGION AND FAITH—
tell me about your:

Faith: _____

_____

_____

Church: _____

_____

_____

_____

A special time in your life where the Lord intervened: _____

_____

_____

_____

_____

_____

Favorite Bible Verse(s): _____

_____

_____

WORK, CAREER AND EDUCATION

What jobs have you had? _____

_____

_____

_____

_____

_____

Were you in the military? _____

_____

_____

_____

_____

College? _____

_____

_____

_____

_____

HOW YOU MET EACH OTHER AND YOUR WEDDING

Special times in your life: _____

_____

_____

_____

_____

Starting a family: _____

_____

_____

_____

_____

YOUR ADVICE TO US

What is the one thing you would want us to know and do? _____

_____

_____

_____

_____

_____

HOW WOULD YOU LIKE TO BE REMEMBERED?

What is the main thing which you want to be known for? _____

_____

_____

_____

_____

_____

_____

_____

_____

_____

_____

_____

_____

_____

NOTES TO THOSE I LOVE

"Letters are among the most significant memorials a person can leave behind them."—**Johann Wolfgang von Goethe**

This is the space for you to write notes to your family:

_____

_____

_____

_____

_____

_____

_____

_____

_____

_____

_____

_____

Tim Fortner

HELP FOR PARENTS AND GRANDPARENTS ON KEY ISSUES

"Then He got into the boat and his disciples followed Him. Without warning a furious storm came up on the lake, so that the waves swept over the boat. But Jesus was sleeping. The disciples went and woke Him, saying, 'Lord, save us or we are going to drown!'" He replied, "You of little faith, why are you so afraid?" Then He got up and rebuked the winds and the waves, and it was completely calm. The men were amazed and ask, "What kind of man is this? Even the winds and the waves obey Him" (Matthew 8: 23-27. NIV).

One of the books in my required reading in the Colson Institute course is entitled, "A Practical Guide to CULTURE," by John Stonestreet &Brett Kunkle, printed by David C Cook, (C) 2017, 2020

The subtitle provides a clear description of its content: "Helping the Next Generation Navigate Today's World."

In the last two years, we have seen a furious storm threaten to sweep us away. We feel like the disciples. Our fears are washing away our faith. Notice when you read the account in Matthew, you have the story of the faithful Roman Centurion, whose faith amazed the Lord Jesus. What kind of faith was this faith, which so amazed the Lord Jesus and caused Him to critique the disciples' faith as little?

The faith of the Roman Centurion was:
- Unselfish faith: he asked for his servant, not himself.
- Understanding faith: he understood authority
- Risking faith: the Lord Jesus offered to go with him, but he said it was unnecessary for Jesus to come in order to heal his servant
- Effective faith: his servant was healed

What kind of man is this? He is the God-Man, God in flesh. Are you afraid of the storms in which we find ourselves? Does it seem to you as if our Lord Jesus does not care? Put your hand in the hand of the Man who stilled the waters!

Let us look at the storms which have engulfed our culture and see how we can help our children and grandchildren navigate through this storm.

A navigator is a person who directs the route or course of a ship at sea—or an aircraft in flight. The navigator uses instruments, technology, maps, GPS, a compass, and even starry skies. The navigator's primary purpose is to be aware at all times of the ship's or aircraft's position. This requires training to develop the skills and know how to use these tools. They must study and practice learning how to use these tools. So must we study and apply God's Word to our lives on a daily basis.

Here is a list authors, Stonestreet and Kunkle have carefully listed in Part Three of their book entitled: PART THREE: POUNDING CULTURAL WAVES. They list eight specific areas, many of which are intertwined with one another. I will list those for you and summarize the action steps we must take. Put on your life preserver first, and then put on the life preserver for your children and grandchildren, for the waves are pounding us as I write these very words.

Here is the list:
- Pornography.
- The Hookup Culture.
- Sexual Identification.
- Gender Identity.
- Affluence and Consumerism.
- Addiction.
- Entertainment.
- Racial Tension.

PORNOGRAPHY

We live in a culture which is obsessed with sex. At the same time, it is a culture of moral indifference with emphasis on rights rather than responsibilities. Add to that the 'screen time' our youth (and adults) spend on smart phones, laptops, I-Pads and the internet and the instant connection to information, visual images and pornography is overwhelming. Pornography is powerful, extremely addictive, and destructive. It is not a matter of when your preteen will encounter pornography. They already have, more than likely. The more critical issue is how they will respond. As a result, we have a porn epidemic more deadly than the COVID virus.

Science reveals those who become addicted to pornography undergo physical changes in their brain, like those addicted to drugs or alcohol. For preteens and teenagers this can be a lifelong problem which can harm marriages and relationships with the opposite sex. Porn creates perpetual shame and guilt.

Sex trafficking and drug addictions often go hand-in-hand. Those who pay for porn are financing the destruction of lives. We live in the midst of a crooked and perverse generation which is creating slaves and destroying lives among our youth. Porn is a killer; it kills marriages, spiritual lives and ruins the gift of sexual intimacy God designed for marriage between a man and a woman.

As a result, sex, marriage and babies have become separable. Men and women have become interchangeable. And sexual freedom has become the epitome of human dignity with cheers for those who are free to become themselves. We are drowning in a storm of sexual immorality.

RESOURCES

Have an honest conversation with your children (all ages). It is not to be an angry or guilt causing a tirade, but a loving, honest conversation to make them aware of the dangers of this ever-present deadly epidemic. Pornography's whole purpose is to create lust. Remember the three prongs of temptation: lust of the flesh, lust of the eyes and pride of life. These are the three which caused the fall in the Garden. 1 John 2:16, 17 tells us: "Love not the world or the things in the world. If anyone loves the world, the love of the Father is not in them. For all that is in the world—the lust of the flesh, the lust of the eyes, and the pride of life - is not of the Father, but is of the world. And the world is passing away, and the lust of it; but he/she who does the will of God abides forever."

Open your family's eyes to the horrific consequences of pornography. Visit the National Center on Sexual Exploitation's website: www.endsexualexploirtation.org. Download their free E-book, "Pornography: A Public Health Crisis. "

Put on your life preservers by placing an internet filtering or monitoring system on your children's smart devices. www.opendns.com/

Net Nanny—www.netnanny.com

Covenant Eyes—www.covenanteyes.com

THE HOOKUP CULTURE

The Hookup Culture is basically sex without commitment, one-night stands, sex, no strings attached. Listen to the lyrics of a popular song in the 1950's recorded by Frank Sinatra. "Love and marriage, love and marriage, go together like a horse and carriage, I tell you, brother: you can't have one without the other. Love and marriage, love and marriage. It's an *institution* you can't disparage. Ask the local gentry and they will say it's elementary. Try, try, try to separate them, it's an illusion. Try, try, try and you come to this conclusion. Love and marriage, love and marriage, go together like a horse and carriage. Dad was told by mother you can't have one, you can't have none. You can't have one without the other!" (written by Sammy Cahn).

This was considered the way things were intended to be, because this is what God intended sex to be when He created man and woman. Certainly not the case today. Sex was intended for marriage between a man and a woman. Sex of any kind outside of marriage is a sin.

The lyrics seem outdated and old-fashioned, but listen to this truth, ' try to separate them, it's an illusion.' All lies from the enemy which are contrary to God's law are an illusion. The enemy is a deceiver. His method always follows the same formula: he minimizes the risk and maximizes the benefits. Sex is pleasurable, it is a natural desire, and God is forbidding you pleasure. This was the enemy's strategy when he deceived Eve. You will not die—a lie. You will be like God—a lie. No consequences? Lost their home, damaged their relationships with one another and with God. Died spiritually—immediately, and physically—gradually.

What are some of the consequences of sex outside of marriage in the hookup culture of today? Sexually transmitted diseases. According to the Center for Disease Control and Prevention, the infection rate of sexually transmitted diseases is on the rise, especially among the ages of 15-24. Chlamydia, gonorrhea, syphilis, and other HPVs are on the rise. The consequences of these are severe: chlamydia can cause infertility and damage to a woman's reproductive system. Others can cause genital warts, cancer and for some there is no treatment. In addition, there is the chance for an unwanted pregnancy which can lead to abortion which has long-lasting impact on mental health.

But even if one escapes any of these issues, permissive sexual behavior can cause problems in marriage later. Clearly, sexual freedom outside of God's instructions is not all that it seems; sin always has consequences. Not that one cannot be forgiven and restored, because God is faithful to cleanse us of all our sins. God's focus from the beginning was on family. The enemy has been trying since the Garden to destroy family and sexual lust and desire misdirected by the enemy has been one of his most successful strategies. It has created the culture of sexual immorality we are witnessing today.

God created sex and it is a wonderful gift for both reproduction and pleasure. Done the right way, God's design brings the joy of sexual intimacy for both pleasure and purpose. Sexual desire is normal. But when you get the cart before the horse, a wreck is sure to follow.

A guide for dating for your children and grandchildren:
1. Never be alone with a date.
2. Stay in public places.
3. Double date—group dates.
4. Don't date exclusively.
5. Teach your sons to be gentlemen.
6. Pray and trust God.

RESOURCES

Free downloable ebook: <u>www.nationalmarriageproject.org</u>

"Before I Do." What do premarital experiences have to do with Marital Quality among Today's Young Adults?

SEXUAL ORIENTATION

When it comes to this matter of sexual orientation, there is a gap which exists between the views of the younger generations and the older generations. Same sex marriage and its twin sister, sexual orientation, have caused many of the younger generation to consider the church on the wrong side of this issue and irrelevant in this matter. Surveys reveal of all the cultural issues this one seems to be sinking the ship of Christianity in the 21st century. Many churches are trying to aright their position, without compromise, but find it a difficult task to navigate.

Society and the media have applauded and affirmed sexual orientation and gender identification, as a personal right to be celebrated. We witnessed this issue come to the forefront on April 13, 2013, when Jason Collins, an active NBA player, publicly came out and announced he was gay. The media applauded and affirmed his choice. Collins received public congratulations from the President and Mrs. Obama for his courage and example. No wonder many of the younger generation think the church is on the wrong side of this issue.

Marriage, as God intended and created it to be, was between a man and a woman for life. Therefore, sex outside of these parameters is a sin—be it heterosexual or homosexual. The enemy with the aid of the internet, social media, entertainment, and propaganda has made the LGBT rights the issue of our times. Many denominations are softening their stance on the status not only of this sexual sin, but all sexual sin. The narrow way is being widened. Give the enemy an inch and he will take a foot.

This is why truth is so important. Remember what Jesus said to those Jews who believed: "If you continue (abide) in My word, you are my disciples indeed, and you shall know the truth and the truth will set you free" (John 8:31, 32). Four verses later, Jesus claims, "If the Son sets you free, you are free indeed." (Notice Jesus uses His name in the place of truth, for He is the Way, the Truth and the Life.

The media portrays Christians who believe the Word of God as true as

narrow minded, bigoted and treating the LGBTQ group harshly. Surely there are those Christians who have mistreated this group, but the media's portrayal as this being the mind-set and attitude of the majority of Christians is overly exaggerated. We are to love our neighbors. Why? Because all people are made in the image of God and we are to honor and respect each and every one with dignity. Jesus even said pray for those who persecute you. As a result of this portrayal of Christians, the gay community has been led to believe the church is filled with hate toward them because of their sexual orientation. Here is the key point: Make Jesus, not their sexual orientation, the key issue. Our priority is not to convert them from homosexuality to heterosexuality, but point them to Christ for salvation.

What about those who say, they were born that way? There is no scientific evidence which has been discovered or verified this to be true. We are all born with a sinful nature. Each one of us is tempted when drawn away by his or her own desires. The enemy has so many buttons he can push through the ever present media, he has temptations of all kinds to lure us and awake a sinful desire. As the saying goes, "Opportunity sometimes only knocks once, but temptation leans on the doorbell." A mind saturated with the truth of God's Word will recognize a lie and use the Word of God to take it captive, as Jesus did in Matthew 4.

RESOURCES

Here are two excellent videos to order and watch from Living Hope Ministries.

Why? Understanding Homosexuality and Gender Development in Males. http://livehope.org/resource/why-dvd/

Why? Understanding Homosexuality and Gender Development in Females—http://livehope.org/resource/femaledvd

Speak the truth in love. Make Jesus the key issue, not their sexual orientation. Learn how to ask good questions. And always be prepared to answer frequently asked questions with well-thought out answers.

GENDER IDENTITY

A statement I heard John Stonestreet make in a lecture is making more sense the more I think about it and observe the culture of the 21st century. He stated: "'Sex, Marriage, Babies—have become separable. Men and women are interchangeable. Be who you want to be, do what you want to do. Complete self-autonomy." All of a sudden, freedom has become the enemy of freedom. It is really simple—too much of a good thing is a bad thing. This mind-set of self-autonomy is now 21st century culture's idea of the epitome of human dignity. This is being promoted as the new normal. Tolerance of this is not enough. You must affirm their beliefs. They want us to approve of those who do these things.

On July 30, 1976, Bruce Jenner crossed the finish line during the last event of the Olympic Decathlon to take home the gold medal in the 1976 Summer Olympics in Montreal. Olympic Decathlon Champions are often declared as the greatest all-round athlete in the World. In 2015, Bruce Jenner took the measures to become a woman, now known as Caitlyn Jenner. He/she was recognized the same year with the Arthur Ashe Courage Award for being ' true to self and in front of her peers'. Glamour Magazine actually declared Jenner, "Woman of the Year." No wonder young people are confused.

Today we celebrate what we once condemned, and condemn what we once celebrated. Evil is called good. Good is called evil. We are as a culture is suffering from "spatial disorientation" which, for a navigator of a plane, is deadly. They cannot tell up from down, and are flying upside down, believing it is right side up. The results are disastrous. It was said of Paul and Silas by the mob which attacked the house of Jason looking for them, "These are the men who have TURNED THE WORLD UPSIDE DOWN and have now come here" (Acts 17). They actually were turning it RIGHT SIDE UP, but the mob viewed it as WRONGSIDE UP!

RESOURCES

Review the DVD's mentioned earlier from Living Hope Ministries regarding Gender identity.

Teach your kids the creation account as how God designed us male and female. This is His order; gender is a gift of creation. Understand psychological problems which need to be addressed with compassion and counseling. Gender dysphoria is a growing problem, but solving a psychological problem with physical sex change surgery is not the solution. The end result will be a feminized man or a masculinized woman. Gender is not a social construct, but the intended design of God who is all-wise and does not make mistakes. Be not deceived.

AFFLUENCE AND CONSUMERISM

America is the land of the free and the home of the ultimate consumer. America is a consumer nation. Consumer spending drives our economy. Affluence also breeds boredom. And when Americans get bored, they go shopping.

Most of my generation lives in a house larger than the one we grew up in. There are now more television sets in America than people. We had one television set when I grew up. A 17-inch screen, black-and-white, was all that we had—and only three channels. No remote control—except my brother and me. We watched television as a family each night after supper. (no TV in the kitchen) We knew what we wanted to watch each night. We laughed, we were entertained, my mother would usually cry, and of course we all cried when Davy Crocket died at the Alamo. We were never embarrassed by its content—no inappropriate sexual innuendo, nudity and profanity. And good always overcame evil. Today, we have 1000s of choices of shows but are completely bored with television and spend more time trying to find something worth watching.

Our culture has redefined the good life in terms of what we possess: house or houses, clothes, automobiles, hobbies, vacations, eating out and the list goes on and on. My grandfather was born in the 1890's, grew up farming. He was the smartest man I ever knew. He worked hard, had his own business with a simple economical philosophy: "If your outgo exceeds your income, then your upkeep becomes your downfall." Simple. Today we consume, and make room, for the new by throwing away the old.

A man's life does not consist of the abundance of his possessions. I have more than we ever had while growing up. But when I think back to those nights when we all sat down together at the dinner table and after supper, did our homework. Then we sat down as a family to watch our regular shows. All of us in our den to watch some wholesome entertainment—which often enforced good morals. It was a simpler life, a good life. But it was lulling us into accepting a stranger in our home, who we thought was good— but a deception was being brought into our lives, which changed our view of reality. Later we realized that, with advertising, we were allowing a parade of idols to come right into our home. We must be careful what we treasure, for where our treasure is our heart will be also.

Ask yourself this question: "Are you wanting your children and grandchildren to have a good life, as defined by a nice house, good education, a spouse and family, a good car, good job, good income, security and significance?" Of course, you would add, we want them to be saved, go to church, etc. Are we really different from the non-Christian who wants the same things? Now Jesus said, "Your Father knows you have need of those things, but make sure your priority is to seek first the Kingdom of God and His righteousness and all the things you need will be added" (did you notice Jesus said "need," not want or desire? Need is a pesky word, isn't it?).

Teach your children and grandchildren how to manage money and avoid debt. They need chores for which they receive an allowance. They need jobs when they reach their teen years. Learn how to budget, tithe, and teach them to give away things regularly to charities or those in need. Money is not evil. The love of money is. Money is neutral, can be used for good or bad. Everything belongs to God.

Encourage them to donate time to a charity. Debt creates problems in marriages and families. If you have struggled with money and budgets and debt, share your mistakes with them. Make very wise decisions about college, preparing for career and real life. The greatest impacts on one's life are the choices we make. Teach them how to make wise decisions and recognize those most important decisions. The Bible is a book of wisdom and God has said, "If any lack wisdom, let him ask of God, who gives to all, liberally and without reproach, and it will be given. But let him ask in faith, with no doubting, for he who doubts is like a wave tossed by the sea driven and tossed by the wind. For let not that man suppose that he will receive anything from the Lord, for he is a double-minded man unstable in all his way" (James 1).

RESOURCES

Dave Ramsey has "Financial Peace Junior: Teaching Kids How to Win with Money."

ADDICTION

The meaning of addiction is a ' strong and harmful need to regularly have something (such as a drug) or do something (such as gambling). The person addicted may know it is harmful but is unable to stop using a substance or engaging in an activity or behavior which is causing problems.

The first step of Alcoholics Anonymous is: "We admitted we were powerless over alcohol and our lives had become unmanageable."

This led to the second step: "We Came to believe that a Power greater than ourselves could restore us to sanity."

On September 16, 1977, I went to my first AA meeting in a church basement in Nashville, Tn. When I walked in, they were reading the 12 steps and I knew the Lord had led me there. I had almost committed suicide that very morning having lost all hope of ever getting sober. I had battled alcohol for 14 years and that morning I had run completely out of hope. Hopelessness is the darkest place on this earth. Hope is the very oxygen of our souls. But on my knees that morning I had cried out to the Lord to save me. He had an AA meeting starting within five minutes of my hotel room, only a half block away. Nothing is impossible for God. I know it for a fact.

The pandemic has really impacted business and more and more we are becoming accustomed to shortages and empty shelves. Sometimes realizing we really did not need what we went looking for—but we are habitually looking for something to fill our empty selves. Like the woman at the well, we want something which will quench our thirst for life as it was intended to be.

Now with marijuana legal in many states and our own government the biggest bookie with the national lotteries, we see vices legalized. But just because something is legal does not mean it is good.

The drug of choice for most teenagers and young people is acceptance. They will try something when placed in a group of peers. Not wanting to appear to be a prude or uncool, they try something which they have been warned by parents is dangerous, for the sake of not being an outsider.

Sometimes we find a truth in a strange place, like the lyrics of a rock and roll song. Huey Lewis had a hit song called "It's Hip to Be Square." Listen to his reasoning in these lyrics: "I used to be a renegade, I used to fool around, but I couldn't take the punishment and had to settle down. Now I'm playing it real straight and yes, I cut my hair. You might think I'm crazy, but I don't even care. Because I can tell you what's going on - It's hip to be square." (Square = Straight, sober, un-addicted and unashamed is hip)

I found a scripture which helped me achieve sobriety. It revealed to me the power of Scripture. I had found a verse in my early days of sobriety. "No temptation has taken you but such as is common to man—but God is faithful, who will not allow you to be tempted beyond that which you are able, but with the temptation will also make the way to escape, that you may be able to bear it" (1 Corinthians 10:13).

The promise is: God will not allow you to be tested or tempted above what you can bear, but will make the *way of escape, that you may be able to bear it.* The way, is Jesus, Who is the Way, the Truth, and the Life. The way of escape is through the problem, not around it. I found myself tempted to take a drink, having just completed 30 consecutive days without a drink. I started praying this promise to the Lord as I meandered aimlessly in my car. Soon I found myself in a cul-de-sac and stopped, and realized in praying and asking the Lord to make a way for me the urge to take a drink had passed.

I learned something important that day. I learned to pray God's word and promises back to Him and to always fight your battles on your knees in prayer. Jesus said, "Come unto Me, all you who are weary and heavy laden and I will give you rest. Take my yoke upon you and learn from Me." That is what I had done in that prayer. I got help with a load I could not bear myself. Yoked with Jesus is where you find a way to bear it. You know who loaded you down with that load? The enemy who told you this is fun; you will be cool and accepted. That day over 44 years ago I learned a lesson I have not forgotten. It is hip to be square; a square is a stable foundation to build your life on—the four square foundation of the Gospel of which the Lord is the key cornerstone. It's hip to be square!

RESOURCES

Find a church with a Celebrate Recovery Program or a local AA meeting or both. Go. Get plugged and get a sponsor. You will never regret it. Get into the Word of God it is the only source of instructions for how to live a life which satisfies your every longing.

ENTERTAINMENT

Aristotle made this observation in 300 B.C.: "Art imitates life." What did he mean by that? Creation of art in its many forms, painting, sculpture, plays, movies, music, are inspired by what the artist sees in the beauty of nature or in a true life story. The artist then conveys their perception of what they have observed filtered through their own thought process and belief system. I loved the artwork of Norman Rockwell. He could paint a scene of life which told a story without words. As you looked, you could imagine what was going on. Modern art which portrays vivid colors and distorted images are of no interest to me.

Oscar Wilde came up with this statement: "Life imitates art, more than art imitates life" (1899). We are influenced by art, movies, books, music in which the creator of the art shares his perception. Quite often, the goal is to influence the person who looks at his painting, reads his/her book, goes to the movie, or is captivated by the lives portrayed in a television series. A few years ago, everyone was following the story and characters of the PBS series, Downton Abbey. Oscar Wilde's statement makes us realize these are powerful tools of influence. They can change the way we view life.

Many movies, television shows, plays, novels, and art are imbedded with a message. A message movie has the purpose of changing the way you think about life and pertinent issues. It is done with entertainment which captures your attention with its story line, characters and the curiosity it creates. In the written word, we began to visualize in our minds these characters portrayed in writing. So these visual images on screens cause us to suspend reality while becoming drawn in by this person's perception of reality. Does it match with the truth of God's Word? How are good and evil portrayed?

Watch "It's a Wonderful Life" and perhaps compare your life to George Bailey's life. He can't seem to get a break. He is a victim of circumstances. Life deals him one bad hand after another. He does not get to live out the life he believed he deserved. Financial struggles and an evil power are portrayed by the villain, Potter. Yet, as we watch this character grow in contentment, we see in the end (as his brother says): "Here is to my big brother, the richest man in town." Life is not always as it seems or how it is portrayed in the arts.

We always knew who the good guys were in the Westerns, they wore white hats, and the bad guys wore black hats. Today it is not that simple or obvious. The media may portray a life described in the Bible as sinful as a hero and may cause you to admire this person and accept their sinful lifestyle. It may be a message movie about saving the environment or the horrors of war, or sex trafficking. These can be good motives, but what are the solutions they offer for the problems they frame?

Have you ever come out of a movie inspired by the character and spirit of the hero of the movie? You wanted to be like them. Who did not love the moment in the movie, "Rocky," when, through his hard work to get in shape and be the best he could be he raced up those steps as the music reached a crescendo? A simple story, even a predictable one, but the hero had things about him that we admired that were good.

Teach your children and grandchildren how to detect a message which is contrary to the Word of God. Do they portray what we know is sin as something which is good, acceptable and even admirable? If the movie is about historical events, are they accurately portrayed? Draw attention to distortions and outright false teaching and lies.

We have all had heroes. People in real life who we admired and wanted to be like. Entertainment can really draw us into a make-believe situation where our emotions are manipulated. The power of influence of the arts and all they encompass is influencing the next generations. Watch television as a family. Do not use television and other screen resources as ' baby sitter' for your children. Get some board games, or go outside for a game. PRACTICE WHAT YOU PREACH!

RESOURCES

Try this Christian movie guide: movieguide.org
Also, see: Axis.org www.axis.org
Center of Parent/Youth Understanding— www.CPYU.org
Read a classic book together as a family.
Take time off from all screen activity. Get creative

RACIAL TENSION

We are told by Jesus in Matthew 24: "For nation will rise against nation, and kingdom against kingdom. And there will be famines, pestilences, and earthquakes in various places. All these are the beginning of sorrows." These events we interpret as signs and indications of what Jesus called, "the beginning of the sorrows."

The word for nation in Greek is ethnos, from which we get the word ethnicity. What is the difference between ethnicity and race? These two terms are often used interchangeably, but they are two different things. Genetically, science tells us there is one race, the human race. According to the human genome project which broke the DNA code in the beginning of the 21st century, our DNA is 99.9% the same and the differences between people account for less than 1%. So we are more alike than different. We were all according to God's Word made in His image and likeness. We are all part of the human family.

As Christians we are told "For you are all sons (children) of God through faith in Jesus Christ. For as many of you as were baptized into Christ have put on Christ. There is neither Jew nor Greek, there is neither slave nor free, there is neither male of female; for you are all one in Christ Jesus. And if you are Christ's, then you are Abraham's seed, and heirs according to the promise. "

Ethnicity recognizes difference between people on the basis of language and shared culture. Culture is an identity with a specific group and nationality. Jews are a nationality as well as Greeks. Different cultures, customs and outward appearances occur to a certain extent. God is no respecter of persons. Race is based on a mixture of physical, behavioral and ancestry, with culture. Cultures tend to conform one.

Kingdoms differ from nations, although they are made up of different ethnicities. Kingdoms also known as realm, countries and nations are a defined geographical area under the rule of a monarch. Throughout history battles and wars have been fought between kingdoms, and cultures played a significant role in wars.

Ethnicities are being politicized by politicians who are always looking to create tribes which are loyal to them by proposing to defend these tribes against cultures which threaten that culture's way of life. Racial discrimination is real, but it is not just an American problem, it is a human problem and has been since cultures have been here.

There is racial and social injustice in our culture. The only solution is the Gospel of Jesus Christ. "For He is our peace, who made us both one, and has broken down the wall which separated us." This is the power of the gospel. We have a spiritual problem which requires a spiritual solution. Do not let your family be unarmed for these critical cultural battles described here.

RESOURCES

Read Martin Luther King's Letter from a Birmingham Jail. http://kingencyclopedia.standford.edu

The Great Commission commands us to make disciples of ALL NATIONS.

Read and memorize this command: "All authority has been given to Me in heaven and on earth. Go ye therefore and make disciples of all the nations, baptizing them in the name of the Father and the Son and the Holy Spirit, teaching them to observe all things I have commanded you; and lo, I am with you always even to the end of the age. Amen" (Matthew 28:18-20).

"Disciple" is not a label. "Disciple" is a lifestyle. Teach it. Model it. Mentor others—starting with your family.

ABOUT THE AUTHOR

Tim Fortner and his wife Gina have been married over 45 years. They have three children and three grandchildren and reside in Hernando, Mississippi, where they are actively involved at Longview Point Baptist Church.

Tim has enjoyed five decades in the vision care industry. In 1989 Tim was involved in the test market of a new photochromic technology. After a successful test market, Mr. Fortner joined the new company which launched the new photochromic technology, Transitions Lenses in 1990. Tim spent the next 25 years traveling worldwide as a speaker, writer, and trainer to over 100,000 eye care professionals all around the world. Tim retired in 2014 when the company was sold. It was by that time a global company and valued at over $3.4 billion. Mr. Fortner also spent four years as Chief of Optical Services at Southern College of Optometry and an adjunct professor.

Tim was well known worldwide as an author, lecturer, teacher, and trainer. He was known for his storytelling as well as his innovative, research-driven insight into patient behavior.

Beginning in 1989, Tim began teaching a weekly, co-ed Bible class. He continues to teach and write. Tim's ministry is concentrated on discipleship. Emphasis is on leaving a legacy for the generations coming behind us. He also has a popular lecture to 14–18-year-olds, called, "The Big Ten," which focuses on those 10 most important years after leaving high school.

A recovering alcoholic, sober for over 44 years, Tim speaks to AA groups and Celebrate Recovery programs. He is a popular speaker at men's prayer groups, discipleship training and workshops. He also speaks to the empty nesters and retirees with vital information and resources for passing on the baton of faith to the next generations. This presentation is based on his book, "UNASHAMED." He is also a popular speaker at reunions.

He is the author of: "The Journey of a Prodigal" a spiritual autobiography about Tim's battle with alcohol. "People Get Ready," a devotional book based on the music of the 60's. And his newest release, "UNASHAMED."

Tim is available for a variety of presentations, workshops with focused teaching and training for the above-mentioned groups.

Books are available online in electronic or paperback via Amazon.

Contact Tim @ 731-426-3459 (text preferred), or johntfortner@gmail.com

Made in the USA
Columbia, SC
07 June 2022

61418017R00059